TRANSITIONS

Stories of Our Journeys

Edited by

Talia Houminer

ISBN: 1-4033-3855-8 (e-book)
ISBN: 1-4033-3856-6 (Paperback)
ISBN: 1-4033-3857-4 (Hardcover)

This book is printed on acid free paper.

1stBooks — rev. 10/28/02

Supported in full by a United Way Homefront grant.

We would like to thank all the young people who contributed stories and artwork for this book. Also, we are very grateful to Melissa Range, Matt Hinton, Mr. Malone (Clarkston High School), Avondale Elementary School, McClendon Elementary ESOL teachers, and Ms. Tottingham for encouraging their students to share their experiences.

For information on this book and other services we provide to refugees and immigrants, you may contact us at:
GMAAC
Resources for Refugee and Immigrant Youth
901 Rowland St.
Clarkston, GA 30021

(404) 299-6646

INTRODUCTION

In reflecting upon the events that occurred on September 11th, some of us feel compelled to place blame on a specific ethnic contingent. Often times, this blame is unfairly placed on the shoulders of innocent children. This is the first instance of war and terrorism with which some of us have come in to contact. However, for refugee children, those events are an all too real reminder that no country is completely free from danger. The United States has been fortunate in avoiding conflict on its own soil, but those who come here to seek peace and solace have been at this proximity to violence before.

Children who have witnessed countless atrocities committed against them, their families, and humanity write the stories collected here. Yet their gentle spirits and lust for life have not been dampened by their plight.

I edited this book because the children who wrote it have made such a difference in the lives of their friends, teachers, and classmates. They have learned to cope in a new country whose customs are alien to them and whose language is foreign. All have left behind their cherished homes, family members, friends, and pets. We applaud their resiliency and their indomitable spirits as they learn to navigate their way around their newfound freedoms.

I hope these stories, poems, and works of art will serve as a bridge between the greater human community and the refugees that play such a vital role in it. Perhaps through a better understanding of their lives, we will foster a deeper appreciation for these amazing children and the countries they call home. Their pursuit of life, liberty, and happiness will always be a reminder that America is truly the land of dreams.

Talia Houminer
Americorps *Volunteer In Service to America
Editorial Coordinator
GMAAC

CONTENTS

AFGHANISTAN

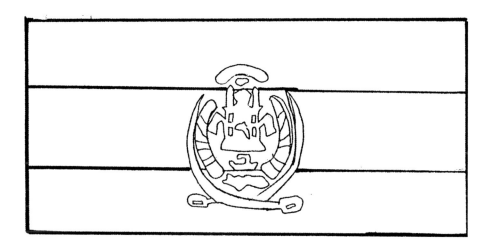

Country Name: Islamic State of Afghanistan

Capital: Kabul

Population: 26,813,057

Official Languages: Persian/Pashtu

Talia Houminer

Hassaina Paykargar

A Healthy Start

My name is Hassaina Paykargar. I am from Afghanistan. We left my country and moved to Russia for eight years. We left because my brother was sick and needed medical attention. Doctors told my parents that it would be in the best interest of my sick brother if they moved to America. We came here in 1999. In the beginning we were sad because we left all our friends.

When we first came we didn't have a phone and we lived in an apartment with lots of trees. We had a friendly neighbor who owned a phone and would let us use it whenever we needed. My first two or three months here I was very lonely. A girl in my class started helping me with reading and writing. Soon we became good friends. I felt much better. Now it has been almost two years since we first came here. I have best friends and good teachers. I am happy again.

Soliman Nadir

A Wish for Afghanistan

The reason that I came to America is because my country had a war. On TV I could see what happened to my country, Afghanistan. I moved from Afghanistan to Pakistan. I have lots of uncles, aunts and cousins there. I have always wanted to meet them. Now I am here, and this place is fun. It is fun because I go to school and meet lots of teachers. I miss my country though. They were in a bad situation. The Taliban had power and there wasn't a lot of food. At this time Afghanistan is free from the Taliban's power. I wish Afghanistan a good future.

Talia Houminer

A. Majeed Hussain

America the Beautiful

Twenty-five years ago, life was very good in Afghanistan. Everyone in my country was happy. They were busy in their life. They had a good life.

After twenty-three years, a war started with Russia. It was a very dangerous war. Many people were killed in that war. Most of them left their country. They skipped from Afghanistan and they went to many different countries. One of them was my family who skipped the country because life was no good after that. It became very hard to spend life in Afghanistan. We came to Pakistan. We thought our life would be better there. After that life became hard in Pakistan. Some people in Pakistan burned our house and our vehicles. Those that burned our stuff didn't like us because we had a good life. They were thinking bad about us.

After that we decided that we should go to a safe place. Then some U.N. people took us from Pakistan. Then we came to America. Now we have a good life like what we had before in Afghanistan. I think life is going to be much better in the future.

BOSNIA and HERZEGOVINA

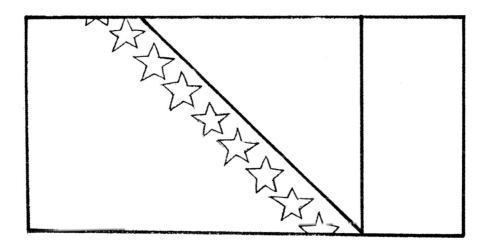

Country Name: Bosnia and Herzegovina

Capital: Sarajevo

Population: 3,922,205

Official Languages: Croatian, Serbian, Bosnian

Talia Houminer

Dzenita Custovic

The Dirty Truth

War! It is a dirty thing, but the war in Bosnia was one of the cruelest wars of all. Can you imagine spending months and months in a vault, wondering when your life is going to end? Every minute is like your last minute. That is what happened to the Bosnian people. Thousands of people are not at rest. Some gave their lives to save the children and stop the war. We won. Bosnia will stand again on both her legs and be what she was before, a beautiful country with a lot of rivers and big mountains. It is a historic place, a place where any visitor can stop and enjoy.

Samir Ominovic,
as told to Amanda Bhame

The Broken House

Where I used to live, people in planes had guns and would throw bombs into our houses. Some people escaped to Germany. They took buses and planes to get there. I was a little baby, only five years old, when I went to Germany.

My dad built our house with tile and he made all the rooms safe. We were in Germany for five years before we returned to Bosnia. When we came back, our house was in pieces because of the bombs. My grandfather sent us a tape of our house because he stayed in Bosnia.

I love my grandfather. He died in 2000. My grandmother didn't care about anything after that. She put on music, and the television, and you should not do that when someone dies. When my family plays the tape of my house in pieces, I go and play. It makes me sad to see all the houses are gone. It also makes me mad that they threw bombs and the houses broke. We got to the United States by taking a plane. I like it here better because there are no bombs and I feel safe.

Fikret Omanovic

Leaving Bosnia

When I was coming to America I did not know where I was going, but my mom kept saying, "Shhh, we almost there." She tell me we are coming somewhere and she close my eyes. When I open my eyes, I saw my uncle and my cousins.

We came to an apartment and my dad buy me a bike. He start to work and my mom and my cousins play darts with me. I learn to speak English and I get new friends. We always play together. In third grade my teacher was Ms. Perry and I was good student. I always did my homework and I learn to play new games.

Alma Keric

A Home Away From Home

It's Monday, April 6,1992, in Ljubija, a small town in the county of Prijedor, Yugoslavia. My mother Dzevida gets up at 6:00 a.m. and prepares for work in a pottery factory called EKK (Elektro Keramicki Kombinat). My father, Kemal, has already left for work in Sanski Most, a town about 20 kilometers away. He works as a manager in a factory called FAMOS (Fabrika Motora Sarajeva- Factory of Motors of Sarajevo). He walks into his office, and as usual, his cup of coffee is waiting for him. Meanwhile, back in Ljubija, I was having breakfast at my daycare center. As the daylight hours slip away, so does the iron bond of communism.

On April 6, 1992, the country of Bosnia and Herzegovina was formed. Until that day, Bosnia and Herzegovina (BiH) was part of Yugoslavia, which was held together for forty-five years in "Brotherhood and Unity" by former president Josip Broz, Tito's iron hand. After Tito's death, Yugoslavia began experiencing conflicts between different ethnic groups, (Serbs and Bosnian Muslims) which eventually led to the breakup of Yugoslavia. After this day, the small but strong country of Yugoslavia would undergo a devastating series of nightmares.

When Bosnia announced its separation from Yugoslavia, conflicts began. The country of Serbia did not want Bosnia to separate from Yugoslavia, and this led to drastic measures. At first, strong dislike was expressed towards the Muslims and Croats from the Serbs. However, over a period of one month, the strong dislike turned into widespread national hatred.

By May 1992, my father could not go to work anymore. The Serbs blocked all of the public transportation and roads to Sanski Most, and as a result, many Muslims lost their jobs. My mother still had her job, but not the same job as before. She had had friends of all ethnicities, Serbs, Croats, and Muslims. Now she was being discriminated against by many of those friends because she was a Muslim.

Three and a half months later, my mother lost her job and the EKK went out of business. During this period, the economy in Bosnia and Herzegovina worsened and all employees lost their jobs. This was the first sign of a national war. The Serbian army started growing rapidly. Fear and panic existed on a daily basis. At this time, I was only six years old, too young to fully understand what was going on. However, what I did understand and remember was that times were changing.

Each day that passed, life got harder. Serbia quickly gained control of seventy-five percent of Bosnia. Almost all of our roadways out of Ljubija were cut off, and we were left stranded in a war zone. The education system changed drastically. Children were forced to stop writing the letter alphabet and had to learn Cyrillic. As the months passed, the tension increased. By the end of 1992, Serbia had started a bloody campaign and ethnic cleansing began.

In September 1992, the county of Prijedor came under the Serbian regime. We had absolutely no contact with the rest of Bosnia or the world. Most of my family lived in Prijedor or in the small towns surrounding it. In March 1993, the Muslims left in Prijedor were forced to move to territories that didn't belong to the Serbs. When this happened, we had no idea whether our family was alive or not, or even where they were. For months we didn't hear from them, nor did they hear from us. Our only means of communication was through letters. However, the Red Cross was under Serbian control, so we couldn't write many things. The Serbs would read the letter and if something they disagreed with was written, they would simply throw your letter away and you would never know.

At first, Ljubija wasn't terrorized as badly as many other cities that the Serbs had control over. It started out simply; any men who weren't Serbs were forced to go to work for the Serbian army. Over time, women were occasionally raped and massive numbers of people were taken to concentration camps. Serb soldiers and police in Ljubija started robbing people. They would break into houses, apartments, and factories late at night, sometimes drunk, and demand all the gold, money, or anything valuable they wanted. If their demands weren't met, they would beat you (men and women) and sometimes even kill you.

At this time, the rape rate went up drastically. We spent every night with one eye open and living in fear. You never knew when the Serbs were going to come and what they were going to do. Eventually, men from all over Bosnia were brought to Ljubia, and into a soccer stadium next to the school. They were tortured, beaten, and eventually killed. The school was right across the street from where we lived, so we could hear everything that was going on. All night long, screams, moans, gunshots, and songs (from the Serbs) could be heard. In the morning, colonies of trucks would pass, dripping blood, and carrying the dead bodies to massive graves where they would simply be dumped. No one talked about this during that time because of fear.

The only food we had was what we grew on our farm at my father's house. We grew food such as corn, beans, peas, wheat, tomatoes, potatoes, radishes, and lettuce. Most of what we grew we tried to sell to make some money, but no one had money. Eventually the Serbian army ended up taking whatever they wanted. People were trying to get out of Ljubija and all of Bosnia. They were hoping to go anywhere. Anywhere outside of the country they used to call home.

My uncle, Osman Keric, escaped to Germany and would send us packages of food. I was never happier than when I saw a little chocolate in the middle of the package. My stepsister sent us a VISA to go to Germany, but we did not have any money. It was very hard for anyone to get out of Ljubija-Prijedor because of the highly armed Serbian army and for fear of your life.

In 1994, my uncle sent us a VISA and money to get out of Bosnia. We left Bosnia on September 21, 1994 and headed for Croatia. On

September 22, 1994, we reached Croatia and had to stay in a UMPA zone. We were waiting for approval to go into an immigration camp in Croatia. The UN controlled the entire area, so for the first time in three years, we were safe. We stayed there for one month until we got approved, and then left for Ivanic, Croatia.

In Ivanic, we stayed in an immigration camp where it was bunk bed to bunk bed. We stayed there for four months while waiting to be approved to go to Germany or any other country that would accept us. The organization that got us out of Bosnia, and was working on getting us to another country, was called Lutheran Services. A man named Fisher ran it. Most of the people that Fisher sent to other countries ended up going to Germany, so we weren't really expecting to come to America. When we found out that we were going to North Dakota, the same state that my uncle was in, my parents were overjoyed. We were finally getting out of the war zone, but we were just as happy that we were coming to America.

On January 16, 1995 we left Croatia. My parents had to say goodbye to the country they loved so much. The country they grew up in, the country where they had built their dreams and expected to raise me. Bosnia-Yugoslavia, the country they still couldn't let go of.

A day later, we reached Fargo, North Dakota. We saw family we hadn't seen in over four years. We saw peace and understanding. We saw breathtaking views of a small American town that we'd never seen before. Most importantly, we saw opportunity and a fresh start. I started 2nd grade in Fargo. I spoke no English and neither did my parents. I had to go to school and make friends with people I could not understand. My parents had to start new jobs and learn a language they had mostly heard in movies. We had to get used to the whole scene in Fargo: busy highways, living downtown in a tight security building, and needing transportation to go to the grocery store. It was like a different world - a different, cold world that my parents didn't like very much.

Six months later, my parents decided to move to Atlanta, Georgia, because of the weather and better job opportunities. When we got to

Atlanta (Clarkston), we had to get used to everything all over again-location, climate, culture, transportation, and language. Neither I, nor my parents, had learned English very well by the time we came to Clarkston.

In Clarkston, I started 3rd grade at Indian Creek Elementary. I was the only Bosnian student in my class, and within three months I spoke English fluently. Since then, I have been an honor roll student, active in extracurricular activities, and have taken an interest in music, writing, and journalism. I have made new friends of every background, and now Clarkston is my home.

I have vague memories of Ljubija and Bosnia. Someday I would like to go back and see where I came from. I would be lying if I said I didn't wish the war hadn't happened. Everyday I feel like something is missing from my life. There is a hole in my soul that can't be replaced with anything I have here. When I look past that hole, I find another hole already repaired. It's repaired with everything that Atlanta has offered me. Although I wish I could go back and change the way things went, stop all these people from dying and suffering, all those women from being raped, and all those men from suffering in concentration camps, I see that it's too late for that.

Clarkston is so diverse that it has given me many things that I never would've experienced in Bosnia. I admit I take it for granted, but when I think about it, I feel overwhelmed. I guess I'll never be able to fill that hole in my heart that got ripped out when Yugoslavia fell apart. Strangely, I feel that if the war hadn't happened, there would still be a piece of my heart missing- the piece of my heart where my "North American dreams" are nestled in a blanket of opportunity, encouragement, freedom, and peace. Clarkston is my home now and here I will thrive and endorse peace. Bosnia is still in my heart. My country is a truth that I will use to tell people, "don't let this happen again…anywhere…ever…please."

Mirnes Sinotic

Bosnia

I came to America so I could work; my father didn't come for himself, he came for me. My country is good because everybody is working, and in my country, people are good at playing soccer and basketball. In my old country, there is fighting in the restaurants. How can we play a soccer game, and basketball, when everybody is fighting? I don't like fighting because you fight one boy and then two people are fighting you back.

Adema Tenik

Unrest Everywhere

In my country there was a war going on. It was hard for my family to stay in Bosnia. The war was from 1992-1995. Much of my family died in the war. I came to America because of the war and my family didn't have a job. People in Bosnia were dying and they didn't have any food. I was a little girl when the war was going on so I don't remember many things. I just know that I saw dead people around me that night when the war began.

My family was afraid to stay in Bosnia because everything had changed. People were mean to you. In Bosnia you were always fighting; you didn't have peace. Everything was expensive and people didn't have jobs. If you found a job, you would get paid three dollars for one hour, and people can't live with little money like that. If I had stayed in Bosnia, I would have nothing, my family wouldn't have a job, and we would have nothing to eat. I wouldn't have nice clothes. I am afraid to go back to Bosnia because everything has changed. I like it here in America. My family has a job, I go to school, and we have peace. But I want to see my family in Bosnia. I wish they can come to America, too.

Talia Houminer

Rehema Zusi

Alma Durak

I Wish to Return

In 1992, war started in Bosnia. I was six years old. At the beginning of the war, Serbs took my dad to camp and he stayed there for five years. My mom, my sister, and I stayed in the city. While war was going on, my uncle was killed. Later on my grandparents died. My mom was working really hard to support my sister and me. We didn't really know our father was in a camp; we all thought he was dead. After the war ended he returned home. His return was a very happy and emotional time for the whole family.

16

We stayed and lived in Bosnia for six more years, which seemed to us a long and hard life. My parents lost their previous jobs and there was no other way to make money. This reason led to the decision to move to the United States of America. My cousin sent us the papers we needed to come here. At first I was so happy to be able to come to America. I thought that there my parents could get jobs. But now that I am older I have come to the conclusion that my life is getting worse here. I always tell my parents that if they want me to be happy, they should send me back to Bosnia. In America everyday you have problems. When you straighten out one problem, another just comes your way. While in Bosnia we were really poor, and my mother couldn't even get food. Now that we have been in America long enough, we have saved some money to support our family if we go back.

Sometimes I think it is better to be poor than to be rich, because money can make people become selfish. Some Bosnians think they're all that because they have money, so they don't have to go back. But I wish I could go back to Bosnia, even if it means I will become poor.

Sefika Hudzisul

Underground Escape

The reason why I came to America is because, in my country, the war was starting. When I was four years old, we celebrated my birthday in a big hotel. When my birthday was over, my mom's friend asked her if I could go with her, just for one week. Then my mother heard on the news that there was going to be war in Bosnia, so my mother told her not to let me come to [my mother] because it is too dangerous.

I stayed with my mother's friend about five years. After that the war was over, a few people told my mother, "if you don't like your apartment house, we going to kill you and take you to the camp." My mother went to camp for nine months. They didn't have any food to eat, so my mother was eating the grass. She was sad that I lived in a town far away.

Three kilometers away was another city where the Serbian people were living. They threw a bomb at my house and I was very scared. We had to go the basement because if the bomb was going to hit the house, it wasn't going to hit the basement. Then after that, my mother came from Bosnia to another town to see me.

When I came home from school, my friends said, "Your mother is here!"

I said, "I don't think so."

Somebody told me she had died, and somebody told her I had died. I did not. When she came to me, I knew it was my mother. I cried all night. I was so happy. I couldn't believe it. Then we made the decision to go to Croatia. When we went to Croatia, I was very happy because my aunt lived there. I lived there for about two years. Then we made the decision to go to America because it is nice and has nice people. Here it is better than Bosnia. I like America.

BURUNDI

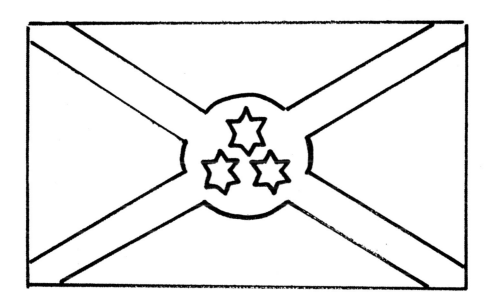

Country Name: Republic of Burundi

Capital: Bujumbura

Population: 6,223,897

Official Languages: Kirundi/French

Talia Houminer

Gabriel Nzabonimana

I Will See God

My name is Gabriel Nzabonimana. Nzabonimana means, "I will see God." When I was in Burundi, I was about three years old. There was war in Burundi. Burundi is a very small country.

There was a war between the Hutu and Tutsi tribes. The war was if they ever see you, even if you are an innocent person, they don't care, they are going to kill you. And there they didn't kill you with a gun. They were going to kill you with a knife and it was pretty scary. So my family and I had to go somewhere that has freedom. We waited until midnight to escape from Burundi so the soldiers wouldn't kill us. When it was midnight, we traveled all day long. It was my cousin, four brothers, my sister and me.

We went to the country of Tanzania. There were many refugees from Burundi and Rwanda. But still, it was not good. We had to beg for food. Every week we had to go get some food so we could live. Every Sunday we went there. It was not only us. There were more than three hundred people who were waiting for food. We didn't have clothes either. So American people came and brought us clothes they had already worn. Sometimes they get some from the trashcan and bring them for us. Also we didn't get to go to school, because if you didn't have money to pay for school, you were not going to go to school. So we, my brothers, sister, and I, didn't go to school.

The time was about 1996. We didn't have food and the food they gave us was nasty. So I got sick. I was sick pretty bad. I became very skinny. Also the bad thing about that time was my father was going to leave us. He was going to Uganda. I was still very sick, so my father told my mother if I died, she should dig a hole and throw me in there. So I was very scared at that time. The only thing I had to do was pray to God. My mother was the only one who helped me at that time. My hand was as skinny as a pencil. You couldn't see my

20

body if you were far away. Everyone had already lost hope and thought I was going to die. Even me—I already said that I am going to die. But God was with me all the time and every second. Finally about two months later I could walk. So I was very happy because my father was wrong. That is how I got my name, Nzabonimana.

A few years later, one man came to our house and told us that if you wanted to go to America, you have to go every morning and see the American people who were helping refugee people. The Americans will ask you many questions. Many people went there every morning but many of them failed the test. We went there every morning. They asked many questions. The people who failed the test and had money would give the American people money so they could go to America and have freedom. But my family and I didn't have to pay because we passed the test.

When we came to America, we didn't speak any English so the people who help refugees helped us. We went to school, my brother and I. I am happy now because I am free to do almost anything I want. I speak English now. So that is not a problem I have. But still I miss Tanzania. But I don't miss Burundi. I wish I could go back to Tanzania, but I would miss my friends.

Rose Mugisha

Escape from Ethnic Battles

My family's story is very long and terrible. The cause of all of this was the war between two ethnic groups. The beginning of the war started in 1993 when the Tutsis killed the first Hutu President, Melchior Ndadaye. The Tutsis killed both the newly elected Burundi president and the Rwandan president by crashing an airplane. This started the war in both countries again, and now Rwanda and Burundi have the same problem. Because of the clashes between the Tutsis and the Hutus, the country stayed without a governor. The war became bigger and bigger.

My uncle looked like both ethnic groups, so if he went to one side, they would try to kill him, and if he went to the other side they would try to kill him. So one day they caught him, and they put him in jail, but that time they didn't kill him. So when he left that jail he decided to go to Nairobi. He lived there for about a year, and then he tried to get us there, too. My aunt began to think about it because our situation was not good, so she started to keep money for the plan of going to a new country.

My family's situation was very dangerous because my aunt was killed by people who put poison in her juice. She drank it with her children and neighbors, but out of all those people, she was the only one who died. My uncle was sleeping in the house that night when someone came and took him away. We still don't know where he is.

After that we started our journey. We went to Rwanda, Uganda, and then to Kenya. We lived in Nairobi for two months. My aunt started the process of coming to America; she kept asking for entry, but it took a long time for us to be accepted because we had to pass many appointments and interviews. When we were living there, my aunt didn't have a job and so me and my sister couldn't go to school.

On March 19, 2001, we came to America and started going to school again. My aunt got a job, too. Now our life is much better.

Navane Babona

Thank You

My family came to America because there were too many people fighting in Africa. Sometimes I thank Jesus because he knows why he brought my family to America. Thanks to my God, bless Africa. Thank you Jesus, you are beautiful. In Africa, my mother and my father are called different names. We call father "papap" and mother we call "maman." I miss my best friends. If you want something, like a camera, I will bring it to you. Navane Babona is a nice girl. If you see her, you'd be happy. Thanks ESOL.

CONGO

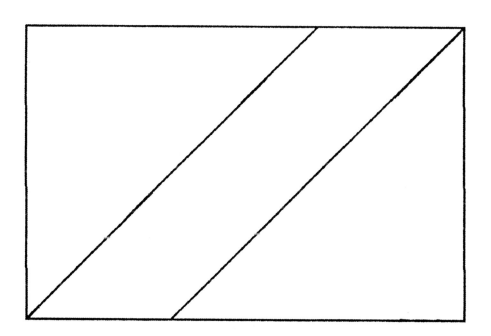

**Country Name: Democratic Republic of the Congo
(former Zaire)**

Capital: Kinshasa

Population: 53,624,718

Official Language: French

Jeannette Kajinga

Why I came to America

When I was in my country, Congo, my mom and dad told me that there were people who were trying to take over. I said, "But why, mom?"

My mom said, "There are many people trying to kick us out of our house."

"But we have a happy family here," I said.

Then we moved to a country called Uganda. We found a house and stayed there for two years. The people that took over my country killed my father.

After two years, some people helped us come to America. For the first time, we had a big happy family again. Many people loved our big happy family and they helped us. Now I live with my mom, my three sisters, and my three brothers.

ETHIOPIA

Country Name: Federal Democratic Republic of Ethiopia

Capital: Addis Ababa

Population: 65,891,874

Official Language: Amharic

Abdisa Lolo
As told to Amanda Bhame

A Losing Battle

I left Ethiopia, and moved to America, because we were at war with Eritrea. Many Eritreans lived in Ethiopia and the Ethiopians didn't want them there. Ethiopians were selling the Eritrean people's stuff, their cars, and their TV's. The Eritreans didn't want to sell their stuff, but we made them. The Ethiopians were tearing the people out from Ethiopia who were not from our country. The people who were turned out even spoke Ethiopian (Amharic). We were scared because we thought our house would be torn down.

We used to go to Eritrean houses to buy stuff. They had a lot of stuff, but it was too expensive. Sometimes a house would be burned down and there would be fights with guns and airplanes. They showed people on TV who were sick and injured. Most were children whose houses had burned down.

In Ethiopia we had a big house with a big TV. A lot of people tried to come to our house when it was dark to take our money. We had a lot of chickens and cats. When we left, I tried to bring my cat with me to Kenya. She was running around and I tried to catch her but couldn't. I don't know if she is still alive.

We were scared that the Eritreans would win, or that Ethiopia would lose the war, so we left for America. I had a cousin who wanted to fight, but I don't know if he did. My grandmother and some of my family are still in Ethiopia and Kenya. My mom wants to go back to Ethiopia. She is still sending money to her friend so her friend can build a big house.

Sena Lolo

Leaving Ethiopia

My family left Ethiopia because there was a war between Ethiopia and Tigra. On Mt. Aetna there were a lot of peaks. Some have no place to live because their houses were torn up or caught fire.

All of the people were scared and some people and their families had to move to another country to be safe. My family all moved to Kenya and lived there for over a year then we came to America where we thought it would be safe.

When I lived in the country, I left to come to the United States at the age of ten. I love America because I have freedom and people are very nice to me despite the fact that I am from another country. I have a lot of friends and they are always nice to me. I love the school I go to and my home.

We came to America because of the war between the British and the Africans, so we didn't have any freedom. Then we heard that the United States had freedom of will, so we knew that this was the best place for us to live.

Zebiba Ahmed

History of the Oromo Nation

The Oromo are a people from the Horn of Africa. They have been colonized by Ethiopia for one hundred and six years. The Oromo population is between 35-40 million people. They have a rich culture and resources! We are the single largest ethnic group in Africa, next to the Hausa people in Nigeria. The Oromo people have fought for their freedom, homeland, and independence for thirty years, led by the Oromo Liberation Front, or OLF.

The Oromo people are the indigenous people of that region. A long time ago, the Oromo people had their own rules and leaders. They had a democratic system where they elected their political leaders. No one came to power without winning an election. Their president was elected directly by the people. He served eight years, which is one term of office. After that, he retired and became the advisor to the new political leaders.

We came to America to seek freedom because the Ethiopian government doesn't like Oromo people. The government oppressed us. We could not live peacefully, and that's why we left. One experience I had was in May 1991. If I remember correctly, I saw a lot of people begging for their lives when the Ethiopian army invaded my village. They killed a lot of innocent women and children who had done nothing against them or anyone; they just happened to be Oromo people.

For example, one day I was going to play with my friends, and I saw about seven dead people in the water. We just screamed and ran away. I saw one of my mom's friends and she told me that the Tigre army was killing people. That was my nightmare experience. I couldn't sleep the whole night because I kept seeing those dead bodies before my eyes. I had never seen death before and I asked myself, why?

We came to America because they killed Oromo people in front of me and I was only twelve years old. Also, my uncle died, along with the rest of my family, except for my little sister and me. After three months, when we came out of jail, my mom said we were not staying in Ethiopia and that we were moving that night. My dad told us we would go to America.

IRAQ and KURDISTAN

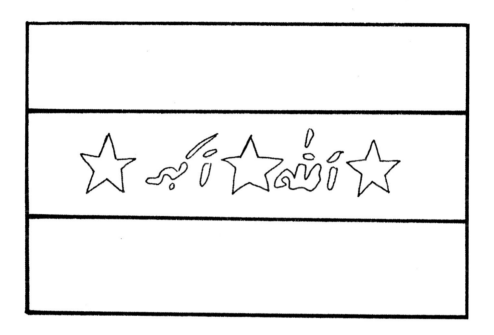

Country Name: Republic of Iraq

Capital: Baghdad

Population: 438,317

Official Languages: Arabic/Kurdish

Fatma Alzerj and Talia Houminer

The Willow Tree

It was a cold and windy night,
but everything felt right.
I scared my shadow off the wall
and followed its path down the hall.
I ran around a corner to see
the most beautiful ever willow tree.

Its leaves were bent in deep lament
and reminded me of the ten years I spent
locked away in a room of rain
rehashing and reliving all my pain.

All my sadness stayed with me,
like the bended branches of a willow tree.
But like the tree, I sprouted hope,
never again to elope
from all my problems and my fears.
When I see that tree, I have no tears.

Fatma Alzerj and Talia Houminer

The Scarf

The silk scarf wrapped around my head
feels like a snake, constricting me with dread.
I have to wear it, because I am made to;
if I had my way, it would be see-through.
If I take it off, all the guilt builds up
filling me with shame, like an overflowing cup.

My mother looks at me as a beacon of perfection;
although she knows I'm not, she thinks I'm her reflection.
I feel sorry for her, but at the same time I'm mad.
I want to live my own life, but then I feel so bad.

She has so many dreams for me, but I also have my own.
Doesn't she understand that her dreams are not on loan?
She didn't have the opportunities that I have, I know;
still, it almost feels as if I'm living in her shadow.

Should I keep the scarf as a reminder of my past?
Or should I throw away the traditions that won't last?
Either way I know that the decision will be mine,
be the scarf on my head, or in my hand, for all time.

Ahmad Rasoul Alzcrj

Reunited

Hi, my name is Ahmad. I am from Iraq. I have a big sister and a big brother who were both born in Iraq. When I lived there, I was only two years old. Saddam Hussein forced my father to go to the army because there was a war between Kuwait and Iraq. My dad and my family escaped to Syria and stayed there for one year.

In Syria, my brother Hasanen was born. Also, my dad's best friend, who was in the army with him, went to Syria to tell my father that Saddam Hussein was looking for him. Hussein had already shot my dad once and my dad's brother died because of the war. So we left Syria and went to Saudi Arabia for two years.

In America, my little sister Zanab was born. We moved to Georgia and went to visit different states like Florida, Michigan, Tennessee, and New York. We left our oldest brother in Iraq because he didn't know how to walk. I was little, and my mom carried me, and my dad carried my other brother. My big sister walked, but my big brother couldn't, so he had to stay with my grandmother and uncle.

My older brother finally came to America a few months ago. He's twelve now. I haven't seen him in eleven years. I was happy when he arrived, and my mother cried. We had a big party, and all our friends came. I gave my brother some money and lots of toys. He thinks America is cool, but he likes Iraq much better. He just hates the war.

Fouad Saleh

On the Road Again

I know something about the *Intifada, so that's why we came
here. First thing, we were in Iraq and it was good and we were happy
every day. My parents, cousins, and family were together, but when
the Intifada came everybody ran away. During the Intifada, we went
to Turkey. It was very cold and we were hungry and thirsty. My
brother and I used to cry. When we got to Turkey we spoke Turkish,
but it's a different language than our language. It was very different
but still we could understand them. So they helped us by bringing us
food, and we were crying and scared. When people help other people
it is very good, and also this helps us. We will never ever forget them.

So, after five or six months, we went back to Iraq because our
stuff and everything was at home. So again the war came. We
moved to Syria and we were refugees and stayed there for ten years.
It was hard to live there, but when my brothers started to work it was
better. After that we came to the U.S.A. We have a better life and it
is kind of good. We are eating and drinking. We are going outside; it
looks like a free country.

*Note: The Intifada is an Arabic word meaning "shaking off." It
was used during the first Palestinian Uprising in 1987 to signify
Palestinian intent to shake off Israeli rule.

Juzan Rejal

My Journal

There were many wars and fighting in my country. This is why I came to America. My dad worked in the army to help the U.S.A. We came here in 1996, and now is the year 2002. We have been here six years. When I came to America, I was so glad that I had peace. America is my favorite country because it takes care of us and gives us more peace on earth. When I was three years old, in Iraq, they were having a lot of wars. My peace on earth wish to America is to be a doctor and have more time to have fun. I can go to school and be a doctor to help people and to learn a lot. My country was sometimes better, but there were too many troubles. This is my journal.

Sharmin Rejal

Sunny Beaches

We came to America because my dad used to work with the American people in Iraq. Then they called our name and they said we have to go to America. My dad used to be a doctor and he was the guard of the hospital. He also used to work on the computer.

Last summer I went to Iraq to visit with my family. When we went there it was very good. We went to concerts, movies and we took trips to the beaches and went to restaurants to eat. I love my country. I wish I could go back there. I might go this summer, but I'm not sure. My mom and dad are talking about it.

Hasanen Alzerj

A Different Life

I was born in Syria. My dad got shot in the war about nine times. He was against Saddam Hussein. We moved to America when I was one year old because it is a free country. We were scared that Saddam was going to shoot my dad a few more times. We didn't even know how to say "bye" or "hi" when we first came to America. We pray on a special mat once in the morning and once at night. We have pictures of prophets around the house.

KENYA

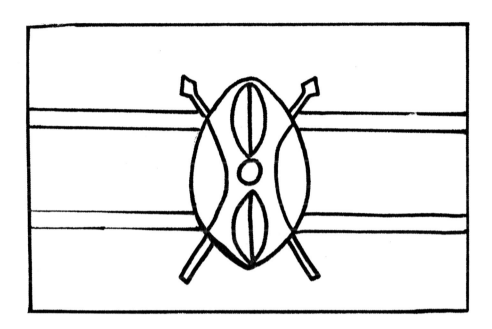

Country Name: Republic of Kenya

Capital: Nairobi

Population: 28,809,000

Official Language: English/Swahili

Talia Houminer

Osman Ahmed

Worms in My Feet

I came to America because there was a war. They were shooting and killing people, so we left for Kenya. In Kenya, we went to a camp. They didn't have water faucets, so we had to use a bucket to get our water. The place was terrible. The worms got into our feet, and some crazy people were burning houses. We had to watch houses burn and people die. It was very sad, so we left for Yemen.

It was better over there. We had a better life. Later, we returned to Kenya. We went to the airport and flew back to the camp. I didn't like it there. We went to my mom's friend's house and lived there. Sometimes we had to carry water. Then we went back to the camp where we had to take a test to go to America. We passed the test and were very happy. We celebrated with a goat. We ate the goat and some chickens. The day came to move to America. We went to the airport and took an airplane. That's how I came to America.

Regine Michelle Zuzi

The World Needs Peace

My name is Michelle, but you can call me Regine if you want to. I'm from Kenya, and I speak four languages: French, Swahili, English and Kiwvando. I'm so glad to live in America because here people love each other, even if you are from a different country. I thank America for their donations, help, unity, peace and kindness. I'm kind of shy and loving. I love my family. I also thank people for their friendship. I thank my ESOL teachers for teaching me English. This land is made for you and me. God bless America.

KOSOVO

Country Name: Kosovo

Capital: Pristina (provincial)

Population: NA

Official Languages: Albanian

Fidan Prenigi

Life in a Tent

My name is Fidan Prenigi. I am ten years old, and I am from Kosovo. We had to leave because of the war and hard living conditions. Yugoslav soldiers who attacked my country threw lots of bombs on my city. They destroyed almost all the houses. Our house was burned down to the ground so we stayed at my cousin's house. I saw many people being killed, and food was scarce. For safety reasons, my family had to move far away. For almost two months we lived in a tent. Many of my countrymen were there too.

There was no school where we were. The children would play outside. Once I got lost and couldn't find my tent. I started to cry. Luckily, a man found me and helped me get back to my tent. After this incident, my mom didn't let me play outside anymore.

by: Qendresa Bushi
KOSOVO Mountain

Florentina Baftija
as told to Christine Howley

The Tractor Ride

One day in Kosovo, a lady called us. It was dark. She said that some people were coming to fight us. My mom woke me up and asked me where my jacket was. I got up and onto a truck. No, something like a truck-a tractor! The bad people threw a grenade at the back and front of the tractor. The tractor blew up, and my dad thought we were not alive. My dad didn't get onto the tractor because he was getting the cows on the farm. Then he saw us, and he was so excited! He gave us some money so we would be safe if somebody came to get us. If someone hated us, we would just give them the money so they wouldn't hit us. They got my mom's things—her dresses, machines and a radio. We didn't hide them because we left too early.

Then we went to a camp. We didn't have anything to eat at first, but then we built our camp and went somewhere to get water. We had to stay there until we went to America, which was a long time. They had to first sign a sheet that said we could go. When we came to America, it was great! Some people met us at the airport and took us in a car to our new apartment.

Arianit Gruda

Arianit's Story

When I left Kosovo, I hid my stuff under the ground and my dad told me that we had to go fast because the Serbs were coming. They took my food and hamburger. They also killed puppies, ten of them. They put mines underground to kill people. They also stole sugar from stores and from people's houses. They were kicking and killing people. They had a big stick and hit people on the back. My dad's brother killed the Serbs because they were being mean to him. They would hit us all on our backs and tell us to act like dogs.

When I went back to my country, I saw a lot of houses that were burnt down. I went in September because it was safe to go back. There weren't any Serbs. I went to fish with my friend. We caught a big fish with a long stick, and I rode a tractor. I lived on a farm and had a dog. I went on the tractor to get something to eat. I bought a little toy car and played with my friends in my new house. They didn't take my house down.

MEXICO

Country Name: United Mexican States

Capital: Mexico City

Population: 99,734,000

Official Language: Spanish

Alejandra Dominguez

The Toy Store

I came from Mexico with my mom, dad, brother and sister. We came here because we were tired of being in the same country. We didn't have money to buy enough food and so we came here so that my dad can work. My mom was working and my dad was too, so we earned a lot of money and we had enough to buy some food!

Mexico is hot; a lot of people live there. I like this country because they have some stores and I like to see stores with toys. My dad brought us here because I was talking a lot of Spanish and my dad was mad because I always talk a lot. So once I got here I went to school, and then I learned English. Every day we go to school in Mexico.

Jose Saldana

Poverty All Around

The reason I came to America is because of the poorness in my country. In Mexico, there is not enough opportunity like in America. My father worked in agriculture, and he had two cows from which he sold milk. My father was the first one to come to America. Then when he was here, he started sending us money. One day my dad decided that he would take us to America. When we told the story to my grandparents, they were sad because we needed to leave them. When we left our house, we were very sad. I was five years old. We got into a bus and left. Then when we got to the border we watched Immigration and then started running and running. When we got to the river a big tire was there. The person who was going to take us said to jump into that tire and the other person will be pulled to that side. When we got on it, the stream was very fast. We got to the other side we started to run, and one of my friends fell down on a train track. Immigration took us to a small jail then let us go. When we got to America, my dad took us to a store and bought us many toys. When we saw the store, it was huge, and we got to see different kinds of toys and bought a lot. Then when we got home, we saw the refrigerator full of food, and I was happy, because in Mexico there wasn't enough. Then we started to live better and better.

PAKISTAN

Country Name: Islamic Republic of Pakistan

Capital: Islamabad

Population: 146,488,000

Official Language: Urdu

Talia Houminer

Belan Esmael

A Hard Lesson

I am from Kurdistan, but I was born in Pakistan. A bomb destroyed our house when war broke out in Kurdistan. We didn't have anywhere to stay, so we decided to move to Pakistan. I completed two grades in a school in Pakistan. I didn't like the way they treated the students. Teachers would punish unruly students by hitting them with sticks. My family soon changed their mind, and we decided to move to America. I went to school, but I didn't understand the students or teachers. Now I know English.

SOMALIA

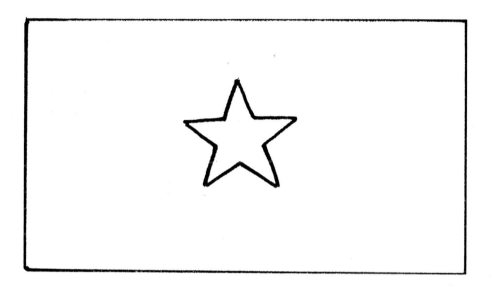

Country Name: Somalia

Capital: Mogadishu

Population: 7,141,000

Official Language: Somali

Talia Houminer

Ahmed Haji

Flowers and Cricket

I am from Somalia. Some people started burning houses, but before they could burn ours, we went to Pakistan. In Pakistan it was peaceful. I learned how to speak English and Urdu. We used to have flower contests, and I learned how to play cricket. In cricket, my favorite player is Wasim Akrim. When my grandfather went to India, he brought me back some pictures of cricket players. I was in Pakistan for six years before my father came to America in 1998. After two years, we came to America. Now, I have been here for almost one year and I am fasting today.

Zulekha Aweis Abdul

The Long Journey to Peace

My name is Zulekha. I am fourteen years old and in the seventh grade at Freedom Middle School. I was born in the desert city of Mogadishu, in East Africa. Unfortunately, I only lived in Somalia for two years before a civil war erupted. Though I don't remember much of it, I can see the sadness that my family feels when they talk about the war. They hold back their tears, but I know how devastating it was for them.

Two weeks after the war started, seven men knocked on our door. If we didn't open it, they said they were going to blow it up. My dad opened the door carefully and let them in. They asked my dad for money and jewelry, but he insisted that we didn't have any. We had already been robbed the night before, but obviously they didn't believe us. Two men took my dad into the kitchen, and another man took my mother onto the porch. One man pointed a gun at my sister and me. The fifth robber searched all over the house, but couldn't find anything.

They demanded that my dad give them money and told him to open his mouth or they were going to put bullets in it. My dad refused, so they hit him on the back with their weapons until he collapsed. My mother begged them to leave her husband alone, but they ignored her. Finally, the screams of my mother alerted a neighbor who called for help. Three Somali soldiers arrived, and the seven men ran away. My parents decided they had to leave Somalia. They kept hoping things would change, but it just got worse.

We moved to Kenya, which is also a part of Eastern Africa. Getting there wasn't easy. We had to walk about fifty miles just to catch a bus that would take us to the Kenyan border. Just when we thought we were finally safe, the border authorities told us we couldn't enter the country because we were refugees. They made us stay in a nearby camp. For the next thirty days, we stayed at the camp. There was no food and no beds. We had to sleep on plastic sheets. Though it was not what we had expected, it was better to be in a place where no one would hurt us. People brought us grain, rice, and fresh water, which we ate and drank over and over again.

Out of nowhere, my father's brother arrived. He told us he had come to get us. That was the happiest day of my life. Somehow he managed to get us to Kenya. We stayed at his home for three months till my father found work as a tailor. We finally got our own place and started a new life. Now my father's brother is dead, God bless him.

We stayed in Kenya for seven years and then got sponsored as refugees. We moved to the United States and now have a place to call home again. Eleven years have passed since we left Somalia, but it is still the same. I will not forget my nationality. Now that we have passports, we don't seem like refugees anymore.

Ilham Ahmed

Ruthless People

In 1992, there was a war in my country. By that time, I was six years old. All my family was alive, and they did not take all our stuff. They just took other people's stuff because we told the killers that we were from a different country. After that we were hiding in some place so that they could not see us. If they saw us, they were going to kill us. They killed one of my brothers in the war, because he was a soldier for one year. By that time, we stayed in our country because they did not take anything from us. We came to America because they were killing a lot of people that did not do anything. They killed the people because Tigre people don't like Oromo people. They even took my brother-in-law to jail. They thought that he was sending money to the people that they didn't like. In my country, when you take a person to jail, they hit you so badly and kill you. If you tell them a lie or if you don't' tell them the truth, they will kill you and hit you so badly. After we saw what happened to the people, we took a bus and went to Kenya. In Kenya the people were nice to us, but the police were bad. They took money from our people. After we stayed in Kenya for eight months, we came to America.

Talia Houminer

Fatima Mohamed

Rowing to Safety

I came to America because there was a war in Somalia. When I was born, the war was just starting. We lived in such a big house during the war, but soldiers came and destroyed the place. The reason for the war was because some people wanted a president and some did not want a president.

Because of all the fighting, my family and many other people rowed a small boat to try and find safety. Three whole days had passed and we were without food. One day, while we were on the boat, one woman said, "I can't live like this anymore." The woman decided to kill herself by throwing herself in the water.

We finally got to Kenya, where my family and I shared a small brick house for five years. After Kenya, we were then taken in an airplane to America. In America I go to school now and have an apartment, and I'm now in the fifth grade. I have been in America for six years, and I really like it here.

Abdalla Hasi-Mohamed

Beaten Down

My family came to America because of daily life, because of war, because of political classes. My father was a businessman, and he used to bring spaghetti from Italy. The last time the war broke out, my family fled from Somalia and we came to Kenya. My father had two wives; my step-mother got killed in front of my face and they beat me with the butts of the gun. They beat my mother in front of my face, and they killed my baby brother. My mother, she was pregnant, and that baby is now dead, too. They took all the money that we had and they went away.

My father came home and saw what had happened. He saw the blood on my face, my mother who was bleeding, and my stepmother dead. My mother was alive and I was alive, too. We were taken to the hospital and we got better.

We came to Kenya. My dad had to leave behind his business in Somalia, so that all the money was finished and all that business was finished, and all that we came with they took. We had houses in Somalia that were taken away. We stayed in Kenya for ten years, and I went to school there up to eighth grade. I didn't have any money to go to high school, so I had to work and it was not good work, but at least it was better. That is why we came to America. Thanks America.

Ahmed Jibril

On the Run

Many years ago, a war started in my country. I was only seven years old when the war started in Somalia. The war began at 3:00 in the morning. At 12:00 noon my mom took us to my aunt's house. My mom said that we will stay here for a while, but the problems did not stop. We were in Mogadishu at that time, and my mom said we do not want to be here any more since we had been here for seven days and the problems did not stop.

My mom decided to move to my uncle's house which was in Kismayo. My uncle was a governor in Kismayo. We moved there, and it was a little better than Mogadishu at that time. The clan called Haweye was killing people and wanted to be the president. Then they captured Kismayo, and our house was one of the first houses they got in to. They took five cars from my uncle. Days later, they started saying to us, "Which clan are you?" and we started telling them the name of a clan they were friendly with. We could not stay in Kismayo because someone told us that a group of strangers were going to come to our house and do whatever they wanted to do. My mom said to my uncle that we could not stay and that we needed to move to Kenya.

Ayan Sheikh and Khadija Sheikh

A Dangerous Life

We were born in Somalia. We left our country because of the civil war. At that time, our family decided that we needed to leave Somalia. We got to Kenya by airplane. Our uncle paid for the trip. Our uncle's friend met us at the airport. After that, he took us to an apartment where we would live. It was like a little hotel. We lived there for about a year. Then we moved to Mombassa in the same country.

The Somali government didn't let us go to school because we weren't citizens. After living there for only two weeks, police broke into our house. They thought we were part of the I.B.K, a group of Arab and Kenyan students that had been burning cars, fighting with the police and causing trouble. We told the police that we were Somali. They said that if we were Somali, why weren't we in the refugee camps? They told us we had to go to the refugee camp or they would come back and arrest us.

We lived in the camp for two weeks and then left because there were fires going on all the time. There were no fire-fighters, so when a fire broke out, people would have to go and wake their neighbors to put out the fires. There was also no running water; we had to go out and get it from a well. The camp was full of malaria, and many people died. People also died because coconuts fell on their head. Sometimes the coconuts would fall through the grass roofs and onto people while they were sleeping. We moved back to the city and lived in an apartment again.

It was dangerous in the city because if the police saw our boys, they would arrest them for not being citizens. Soon we signed up to go to America. Every time they called us, we had to pretend that we lived in the refugee camp so that we wouldn't get into trouble. They called and interviewed us three times. The third time they let us come to America. We still think about Somalia, our home country. Someday, when there is peace, we will go back.

Salado M Hodan Hirmoge

Why I Left My Country

I am from Somalia. It's a country in East Africa. I've been in America for five years. I came to America because in my country there is a war going on. After we left Somalia, we moved to Kenya. We moved to an area where they had other Somali people. I didn't like living there; the conditions were hard. Getting water was hard because we had to wait in long lines until the water started running.

Somalia was once ruled by Italy. They fought to get their independence and finally did in 1960. I wasn't born yet, but I heard from my family how it was. Somalia was an independent country until the war broke out in 1990. The president of Somalia died and the country fell apart. The civil war in Somalia is not religious. It is about different ethnicities that live in the country. Who knew that Somalia would fall apart? The nation I love has been destroyed.

Some people fought hard for Somalia to become an independent country, while others destroyed their own country and killed their own people because they were from a different ethnic group. I wish to go back to my country one day. I was little when I left Somalia. That was the saddest day of my life. Being told to leave your own house and what you worked so hard for is terrible. How would you feel if a gun was pointed at your head because you didn't want to leave your home?

I came to America for a lot of reasons. Two of them are education and freedom. I am glad to live with my family and still be alive. My family decided we should come to America so we could have a good education and live a better life. I will never forget what happened to my family. I remember being told to get out of the car and get in line and bad people took our money and jewelry and they left us there. Some people would do anything to come to America and I am glad to be here. Why do we kill each other, why do we go around and kill innocent people who didn't do anything to us?

The word freedom means a lot to me. Freedom means freedom of speech, freedom of religion, freedom means everything to me. I had freedom in Somalia before the war. The people who did this don't care about themselves or anybody. They just do it for fun. War is not the answer. If they knew the word freedom they wouldn't do this. I would love to go back to my country Somalia. I don't want to forget my history and culture. Other nations don't care about Somalia or their people.

I came to a country where I didn't speak their language and it was very hard to learn it. I never thought I would come to another country. It very hard going to a different country and growing up around people you don't know.

For me, the first hard thing I faced in America was going to school my first day. I didn't speak English at all, and when the kids around me talked, they sounded funny to me. A couple of months passed, and I spoke a couple of words. I'm saying this because I was living in a peaceful world, when suddenly, war broke out and we were forced to leave our house. Now that I live here, I'm getting used to American culture.

Iqra Diriye

Did We Really Have to Go?

I was born in Somalia and lived there until I was nine years old. I left Somalia because there was a war and people were killing each other. My mom died when I was one year old, so my dad took care of us. One day, my dad took us to our aunt's house. He told her that he was going to come back for us in a month, but he didn't. My dad went somewhere, but we don't know where he is even now. So, my aunt takes care of us. Before I came to America, I went to Kenya. I was there for two years. I like to talk about my country. Somalia was big and beautiful before the war messed it up. It became a rough country. So, it isn't a good idea to stay there.

Nadir Ismail

Deep in the Forest

Hello, my name is Nadir Ismail and I am here to tell you something about Somalia. If you take a look at the map, you can see that Texas is bigger than Somalia. I refuse to live in a place where it's all forest. When I was a farmer boy, my job was to let the goats and cows eat food in the forest. My family lived in the city. Only my grandmother and I lived in the forest. In the forest, I saw many different animals: huge pigs, and lions, which I could not get close to.

Sara Amin

The Cool Trip

My name is Sara, and I am from Somalia, which is in Africa. When I was a refugee in Kenya, they brought us food, like oil, flour and bread. When they were bringing something like that, the people were so happy, they would wake up at 6:00 a.m, and get in line for the food. Then there was an office where people get to go to America if their name is on the list. So one day was the happiest for our family's life because our name was on the list. The night before we were coming to America our friends were happy, but on the inside they were sad at the same time. When we came to America it was fun, and we rode four airplanes, so it was pretty cool.

Abdimajid Abdirahman

The Boarding School

My name is Abdimajid and I am from Somalia. Actually, I am from Somaliland, in northern Somalia. My country is divided into two parts, the northern, Somaliland, and the southern, Somalia. I lived in both parts, mostly in Somaliland. Hargeisa is where I was born, and it has been the capital of Somaliland since 1992. I lived with my family, but our lives were as poor as hell.

My brother and I were in a boarding college called Dalinta Kacaanka in Hargeisa. We were there for seven years. It was horrible. We ate beans, peas, and junk food. There were no good foods. We lived in a room with twenty kids. We visited my mom every Friday to Saturday, where she would change our clothes and give us good food. It was like living in a place where we were slaves. I used to cry many times alone and my tears would wet my shirt. It was like nothing else because we couldn't leave there. I mean, we could, but where would we go?

My mom lived alone and she used to sell foods so she could have something to give us when we visited her. I forget to mention, but my dad tried a million things to make our lives better. After a while, he went to Saudi Arabia illegally. Then he got a VISA from someone he knew in the United States. Finally he came to America but couldn't find a job for a long while. Then he got a job and he used to send us money. Then he applied for a VISA for us, and after he raised our ticket money, we came to America in the hot summer of 1999. And now we live better than ever!

Regine Michelle Zuzi

AFRICA PEACE

UMOJA
PEACE

Abduladif Said

Just a Short Ride Away

My name is Abdul Said, and I'm from Somalia. In this story I want to tell you about my worst life in Somalia. At that time, I was three or four years old. I couldn't play soccer with my friends because there was war outside all the time. In Somalia, my mother's friend died, so my mother got mad and said she wanted to move to America. But it was hard to come to America, because you had to sign papers and wait for days and months. So one day we received a letter saying that we had to move to Kenya and stay there. One day an airplane came, and we got inside, and after about three or four days, when we got outside, there was America. America was beautiful. I met some new friends. I went to school and now I am in the 8th grade.

Fatima Awo

Broken Dreams

I was four years old when I left my home country of Somalia. I moved to Kenya and lived there for seven years. When I left Kenya for America, I knew that life was going to change a lot.

I don't know much about Somalia because I lived in Kenya for so long and that's where I grew up. I know much about Kenya. It is a wonderful and beautiful country. I like Kenya better than Somalia.

When we moved from Kenya to America, some of my family stayed there. For example, my oldest sister, her husband, and her children stayed there. My aunt, who is my dad's sister, was still in Kenya. Many of my family were in Kenya and I didn't want to move or leave.

I didn't want to move to America because there was no one I knew who lived here. When we were coming to America, most of us were taken to different states and we thought we were never going to see each other again. I didn't know that we were coming to a wonderful place like this country. I never thought you could move around states in the United States. I thought you would have to live in the same place where they put you.

Life changed a lot in America, but it is better than anywhere else. Everything in America is so different from Africa. For example, the stores, markets, and the way people live are so different, and the way Americans organize their things is different too. We didn't go to school in Africa because we couldn't pay for it. We get to go to school in America, which is so wonderful and we get to be the ones who are educated. Now I am so glad that I came to America and go to school. I have learned a lot by going to school and now I speak almost perfect English. I love living in the United States.

Najma Ahmed

Immigrant

I left the land of my birth.
Why I left, only my parents know.
On the way, flying high above the clouds,
I was excited seeing new things.
The sky was blue and everything seemed right.

I immigrated to the U.S. for a better life.
A new life in a strange land,
but beneath my smile was fear and hate.
I expected so much, but I see so little.

All that I sense is mess and pain.
I thought it would be my salvation
but I found myself all alone.
It is hard to be lonely,
because I left the land of my birth.

SUDAN

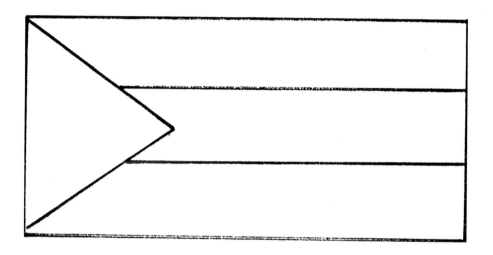

Country Name: Republic of Sudan

Capital: Khartoum

Population: 28,883,000

Official Language: Arabic

Talia Houminer

Wac William
as told to Mrs. Tottingham

Why the U.S. is Just Like Sudan

My name is Wac William. I am from Sudan. We moved here because the people in Sudan were fighting with guns and bombs. A lot of things about the United States are the same as Sudan. When I went to school in Sudan, it was like school is here. We learned Arabic and English in school. We also had some of the same classes, like reading, math, spelling, and P.E. In the United States, I live with my mom, dad, brothers, and sisters. My uncle and sister live in Iraq. I like my school, and I like to play basketball.

Smah Abdelhamid

Health and Education

My family's story is like every refugee story. My country is at war, and that's why we left. The war made us leave because it kept us from having a good education, jobs, and health care. In my country I believe we have the best, the strongest, and the most intelligent school system. We have good teachers and good students. For boys, when they get to college, they have to enjoy it, if not, they will run all the time. It goes on and on and on.

My country is the largest in all of Africa. It's a rich country, and everybody knows if the war stopped, they would start to grow plants, and rice and raise animals. My country is going to be the food basket for Africa, but the war still keeps a lot of people without jobs. Life is expensive. Men are at war, and women can't have jobs.

People need someone to take good care of their health, how they're feeling, and what they put in their body. Health care is one of the reasons my family came here. My father saw how people don't care about health. The night we went to the airport we went to my uncle's. We saw the people who sell food in the street. The kids work in the dirty street. My uncle told me that I was going to the cleanest country on earth, and we would leave the dirty and unhealthy country.

This country is the best education on earth. It has good jobs and good health. Thank you for making me come here.

SYRIA

Country Name: Syrian Arab Republic

Capital: Damascus

Population: 16,033,000

Official Language: Arabic

Wesal Shaban

Leaving

Hi, my name is Wesal Shabaan and my sister's name is Manal Shabaan. We come to the United States from Syria. I was born August 16, 1988 and my sister Manal was born January 1, 1990.

Syria is a beautiful country, and I wish I could stay there forever, but my family felt it was time to leave. We came to the States when I was in the sixth grade, and my sister was in the fifth. We were glad that they allowed us to stay in our same grades and not put us back a grade because school is different in the United States than in Syria.

After being here for a year, we went back to Syria for about two months. Once in Syria, we had to still go to school. I really like school there and it was different from the school I was going to back in the States. The hard thing was once we left Syria again and came back to the United States, they put us back a grade because they said we were not on the same level as the other children anymore.

Now we are in school and our grades are good. My sister and I now go to GMAAC and they help us with our schoolwork and we keep good grades. We are thankful for the people that work at GMAAC.

VIETNAM

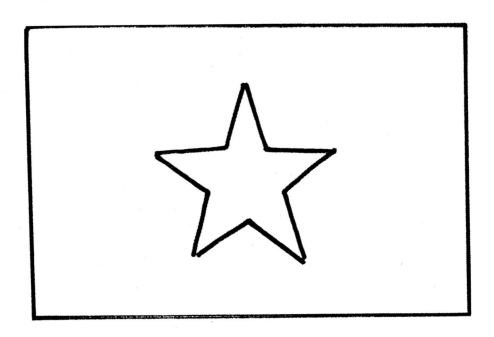

Country Name: Socialist Republic of Vietnam

Capital: Hanoi

Population: 79,490,000

Official Language: Viatnamese

Kieu Nguyen

A Move Toward Survival

My name is Kieu Nguyen and I'm from Vietnam. I came to America because my family was very poor when we lived in Vietnam. There are so many reasons why we came to America. For example, my family didn't have enough money to survive. In Vietnam, my family lived in a friend's house, so we had a hard time living there. We didn't have enough money to buy a house, so we had to live with other people.

In my family, only I went to school because we didn't have enough money to let my two sisters go to school. In my house there are three children. We are all girls. One of my sister's is my little sister, and the other one is my big sister. My family thought to come to America for a better life so they could get a job. That's why my family came to America, and I came also! Bye!!!

Oanh Luu

The Little Mermaid

When I came here I couldn't wait. When I came here, I met a new friend and had a great adventure. I came here to learn and play on the swing. I love to swim because I never swam before in Vietnam. In Vietnam, I was a little girl. I went to swim with my dad there, and my mom was holding me and I kicked someone's leg. I am so glad that GMAAC will be here forever. If it goes away, I will not know where to go. I love GMAAC forever.

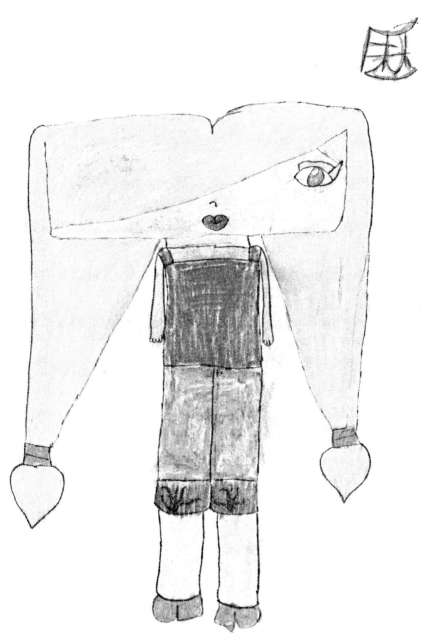

Tuyet Nguyen

Tuyet Nguyen

The Way to Win Friends

Hi, my name is Tuyet Nguyen and I came to America almost ten years ago. My family left Vietnam because the war left my country very poor. Life in America is better than where I came from. I came here to get better education opportunities.

I don't remember much from that time, but I remember how I felt once I reached here. At first it was very scary for me. I didn't speak a word of English and I didn't have any friends. I felt lonely and I cried very often. Now I love school. My favorite subjects are math, ESOL, and science. I made friends by showing respect, and being nice and polite. The best thing about living in America is having cable and watching cartoons. In Vietnam, people don't have cable or cartoons.

Nam Ha

Family History: Journey to the New World

History has shown that many immigrants from all parts of Asia immigrated to the United States in search of liberty. Well, that's basically the reason we strived so hard to escape from our very own country to come to the United States. All we wanted was FREEDOM, which every human being in the world should have, not search for.

After the Vietnam War ended on April 30th, 1975, the country was governed under a communist party. From that day on, citizens of Vietnam suffered dramatically from a lack of freedom, which led to many other dilemmas, such as poverty. Many Vietnamese intended to escape the country for a better place, but got caught and were sent to jail. Fortunately, some managed to make it to the new world and my family and I were some of the lucky few. In the year 1989, we boarded a ship with over one hundred people and traveled to a refugee camp in Hong Kong. We met many difficulties, but we came across it with the help of some friends along the way.

To fulfill our lifetime dream, we never thought of giving up. After living and waiting in Hong Kong for five years, we were finally selected to come to the United States as legal immigrants. The rest were forced to go back to Vietnam in 1998, after Hong Kong was returned to Chinese rule on July 1, 1997. Life was so different after we came to the United States, and that was what we were hoping for. Here in the United States, I am able to go to school with everyone else, without my parents having to pay for it. Discrimination is being practiced everywhere I go, especially in the schools. It's not just a big issue, it's life.

Thuy Nguyen

<u>AFTERWORD</u>

Dear Reader,

We here at the Georgia Mutual Assistance Association Consortium hope you have found this book both informative and inspirational. Since the events of September 2001, there is an even greater need to share these stories. We are privileged to have the opportunity to work with many of these young people on a daily basis. In addition to continual advocacy for the refugee community, we offer a variety of other youth services and programs.

We have an after-school tutoring program, which pairs needy students with VISTA partners and volunteers from the community. We help the children with their homework and encourage them to pursue higher levels of education. Our Friendship Club fosters understanding amongst youth from diverse backgrounds, while our Summer of Understanding and Learning, a summer day-camp, provides the youth with educational and fun activities. In 1994, Students for R.E.A.L. (Respectful Education About Life) was created. This program teaches high school students to conduct diversity workshops in elementary classrooms. It also helps these students to begin breaking down barriers and stereotypes of all kinds.

Because we operate on a limited budget, a large part of our ability to serve stems from our Americorps*Volunteers In Service to America program. VISTAs serve in the community for one or two years and receive a small living stipend and educational award.

They are dedicated to our youth and help mobilize community volunteers and resources. Funds raised from the sale of this book will go directly to the youth program. We appreciate your donation and the investment you have made in the future of these wonderful young people.

Michael Burnham, *Director of Youth Services*

How to Order

You may order additional copies of this book through the 1st Books Library at www.1stbooks.com or you can order directly from GMAAC at:

GMAAC

Resources for Refugee and Immigrant Youth

901 Rowland St.

Clarkston, GA, 30021

Ph: 404-299-6646 Fax: 404-299-6894

ABOUT THE AUTHOR

There is no single author represented in this book. This work is a collection of stories written by refugee youth. The youth are culturally and ethnically diverse. They come from different countries, speak different languages and practice different religions, however, they have all fled their homelands in search of safety and peace. They seek understanding, guidance and acceptance. These children are your neighbors, your friends, your family, and your playmates. They are all of us.

Printed in the United States
795300002B